Riches of the Earth

Potatoes

Irene Franck and David Brownstone

GROLIER

An imprint of Scholastic Library Publishing
Danbury, Connecticut

Credits and Acknowledgments

abbreviations: t (top), b (bottom), l (left), r (right), c (center)
Image credits: Agricultural Research Service Library: 1b, 4, 5, 7l, 9, 14r, 17, 22r, and 23l (Scott Bauer); 8 (Keith Weller), 23r (Jack Dykinga); Art Resource: 12 (Nick Saunders/Barbara Heller Photo Library), 14l (Pierpont Morgan Library, MA3900, f.10v), 15 and 24 (Fine Art Photographic Library); Bettman/CORBIS: 16 (Michael St. Maur Sheil); Getty Images/Foodpix: 11 (Burke/Triolo Productions), 26 (Spathis Miller), 29 (John E. Kelly); Getty Images/PhotoDisc: 3 (Siede Preis), 6 (C Squared Studios), 28 (John A. Rizzo); National Aeronautics and Space Administration (NASA): 1t and running heads; Photo Researchers, Inc.: 22l (Holt Studios International/ Nigel Cattlin); U.S. Department of Agriculture: 7r (Warren Uzzle), 10 (Ken Hammond), 21 (James H. Karales), 25 and 27 (Gene Alexander); Woodfin Camp & Associates: 18l and 18r (C. A. Woolfitt); World Bank: 13 (Jaime Martin-Escobal), 19 (Curt Carnemark). Original image drawn for this book by K & P Publishing Services: 20.

Our thanks to Joe Hollander, Phil Friedman, and Laurie McCurley at Scholastic Library Publishing; to photo researchers Susan Hormuth, Robin Sand, and Robert Melcak; to copy editor Michael Burke; and to the librarians throughout the northeastern library network, in particular to the staff of the Chappaqua Library— director Mark Hasskarl; the expert reference staff, including Martha Alcott, Michele J. Capozzella, Maryanne Eaton, Catherine Paulsen, Jane Peyraud, Paula Peyraud, and Carolyn Reznick; and the circulation staff, headed by Barbara Le Sauvage—for fulfilling our wide-ranging research needs.

Published 2003 by Grolier
Division of Scholastic Library Publishing
Old Sherman Turnpike
Danbury, Connecticut 06816

For information address the publisher:
Scholastic Library Publishing, Grolier Division
Old Sherman Turnpike, Danbury, Connecticut 06816

© 2003 Irene M. Franck and David M. Brownstone

Library of Congress Cataloging-in-Publication Data

Franck, Irene M.
        Potatoes / Irene Franck and David Brownstone.
            p. cm. -- (Riches of the earth ; v. 8)
        Summary: Provides information about potatoes and their importance in everyday life.
        Includes bibliographical references and index.
        ISBN 0-7172-5730-4 (set : alk. paper) -- ISBN 0-7172-5720-7 (vol. 8 : alk paper)
            1. Potatoes--Juvenile literature [1. Potatoes.] I. Brownstone, David M. II. Title.

SB211.P8F793 2003
635'.21--dc21
                                                                                    2003044084

Printed in the United States of America

Designed by K & P Publishing Services

Contents

Some of our favorite foods are made from potatoes. Along with several whole potatoes shown here are potato chips (top left), hash-brown potatoes (top right), fried potato nuggets (center right), a baked potato (bottom left), and mashed potatoes (bottom right).

People and Potatoes

Many kinds of potatoes grew wild and were gathered as food in South America more than 10,000 years ago. In the high country of the Andes Mountains—in what are now Peru, Bolivia, and parts of several other countries—people moved from gathering wild potatoes to planting and growing potatoes at least 4,000 years ago.

Yet people in the rest of the world never even saw or ate a potato until more than 50 years after Columbus discovered America. Potatoes spread to Europe and then to the rest of the world only after Spanish sailors and explorers brought potatoes back home with them (see p. 12).

Today potatoes are an enormous food crop, eaten by at least hun-

This potato expert is holding in his hand samples of wild potatoes. Modern potatoes were developed from tiny wild ones like these. Scientists are studying them to see if they have other valuable properties that can be developed.

cooked as french fries, processed into potato chips, frozen, and dried. Some people even drink potatoes, for alcohol made out of potatoes is used to make vodka. We also use potatoes to feed livestock and in several industrial ways.

Potatoes have also played an unusual role in world and American history. Potatoes proved so nutritious and so easy to grow that they became the main food crop in Ireland and a major food crop throughout Europe. In the late 1840s, when a potato blight destroyed much of Europe's potato crop, Ireland suffered the massive, immensely deadly "potato famine," and much of the rest of Europe also suffered great hardship. That, in turn, triggered massive emigration from Europe to the United States and several other countries, with great impact on their histories (see p. 16).

dreds of millions and probably billions of people. The world's farmers grow hundreds of millions of tons of potatoes every year—and every year the world's huge and growing population eats more potatoes. The world's peoples still eat more wheat, rice, and corn than they do potatoes—but not much more.

We eat large quantities of potatoes baked or boiled, just as they came out of the ground. We eat them

Potatoes come in many varieties, differing in size, shape, color, texture, thickness of skin, and other qualities. Those with thick skins are often good for baking, while those with thinner skins are generally better for boiling.

What Are Potatoes?

Potatoes are the edible part (the part we can eat) of the potato plant. The potato plant is a member of the family of plants commonly known as *nightshades* (their scientific name is *Solanaceae*). Other members of the family include tomatoes, eggplants, and peppers. The scientific name of the potato plant is *Solanum tuberosum*.

The potato plant is a green, leafy vegetable that grows one to three feet tall. The height depends on the variety of potato and the conditions in which it is grown.

As the potato plant grows, it

This is a young potato plant, so small it can be held in a pair of hands. The potatoes will grow from the part of the stem that lies underground in the soil.

Many potatoes today are grown on commercial farms with rows of potatoes stretching to the horizon, like these in North Dakota. The rows are widely spaced to give the plants plenty of sun and air.

uses water and nutrients (nourishing substances) drawn in through its roots deep in the soil. In a process called *photosynthesis*, the plant's green leaves also use sunlight, carbon dioxide (a common gas) from the air, and water to make various *carbohydrates*. These are chemical compounds (mixed substances) composed of the elements (basic substances) carbon, hydrogen, and oxygen. Carbohydrates are a basic part of the cells of every living thing and are necessary to human life. These carbohydrates give the plant energy to grow.

The plant usually has several stems, which grow partly above ground and partly below ground. The underground parts of these stems develop branching substems called *rhizomes*. As the potato plant grows, each underground substem grows a small tip, which grows into a much larger tip and then into a potato. Therefore, each potato plant can and usually does develop many potatoes.

When grown in cool northern areas, potato plants do not flower. But in warmer areas they put out lovely, delicate flowers like these.

Because of the way they look, potatoes and other such tubelike plant parts are called *tubers*. Potato tubers are often mistakenly described as *root plants*, but they are really part of the stems of the plants. Potato plants also have root systems, which are not edible.

The parts of the potato plant that grow above ground, including part of the stems, are also not edible. That is because they contain a natural poison called *solanine*, as do all members of the nightshade family.

One of the most poisonous plants in the nightshade family is the *deadly nightshade* (*belladonna*).

Potatoes grown and stored out of sunlight are not poisonous. However, potatoes that are exposed to sunlight can develop green patches, meaning that they are likely to contain poisonous solanine. That is why potatoes that have turned green or have even small green patches should not be eaten.

The potato plant is usually called an *annual*, because it grows to matu-

This scientist is growing wild potato plants in a greenhouse (a light-filled protective shelter). Such wild plants may have special qualities that can be added to commercially grown potatoes.

rity and dies every year However, potato tubers have many "eyes," growing near their skins. These eyes are really seeds that are re-planted each year to generate a new crop of potato plants and potatoes, so the whole plant is also often thought of as a *perennial*.

What Potatoes Are Made Of

There are hundreds of varieties of wild potatoes, and at least as many more varieties of farmed potatoes. All have the same basic composition, but they vary greatly in the amounts of the substances they contain. Beyond that, such matters as climate, length of growing season, amounts of water the potato plants receive while growing, and the

amounts and kinds of fertilizers used by farmers all greatly affect the substances in the potato.

By far the most widely grown kind of potato around the world is the highly edible, very nourishing white-fleshed Irish potato. Like all potatoes, it is composed of water and solid matter, often called *dry matter*. This is what is left after potatoes have had their water removed, as the Andean peoples did thousands of years ago (see p. 13) and as potato product manufacturers do today.

The many varieties of white potatoes generally contain about 75 percent to 80 percent water. The rest is composed of dry matter.

The dry matter in potatoes is

Though they are called *sweet potatoes* and look much like regular potatoes, sweet potatoes actually come from a quite different plant family. These are sweet potatoes for sale at a supermarket.

made of several main substances. Some 85 percent to 90 percent of the dry matter is made up of carbohydrates. In the potato the carbohydrates include a large amount of starch (75 percent to 85 percent) and smaller amounts of several sugars. The starch and the sugars are major sources of energy.

Potatoes also contain proteins (about 1 percent to 4 percent), which are also basic chemical compounds necessary to human life. Proteins contain carbon, nitrogen, oxygen, hydrogen, and sometimes other ele-ments. There are a wide range of proteins, all largely made of special substances called *amino acids*. Potatoes contain almost all of the amino acids that humans need to stay alive.

Potatoes are also a good source of several other substances important to health. They are an excellent source of vitamin C and a good source of the three B vitamins: niacin, thiamin, and riboflavin. They are also good sources of iron, magnesium, potassium, and several other minerals.

Like sweet potatoes, yams are often cooked with sugar added to their natural sweetness, as in this dish of candied yams on a Thanksgiving table.

Sweet Potatoes and Yams

Two other kinds of edible tubers are often mistakenly called potatoes, but they are not really potatoes at all. One is the *sweet potato* (*Ipomoea batatas*), which is part of the morning glory plant family.

Sweet potatoes originated in the tropical regions of Central and South America, later spreading to other parts of the world, including the United States.

Sweet potatoes come in several varieties. In size and appearance, some of these look very much like common varieties of potatoes and are easily mistaken for potatoes. However, those sweet potato varieties most often eaten in the United States have yellow or orange flesh, though some varieties have white flesh. Like potatoes, sweet potatoes are often baked or boiled. However, unlike potatoes, they contain substantial amounts of sugar and are often candied (cooked with added sugar).

The *yam* (*Dioscorea*) is another kind of edible tuber that is sometimes mistaken for a potato. However, yams are far more often mistaken for sweet potatoes, because of their size and appearance. Beyond that, the flesh of some varieties of yam is orange, making yams look even more like some sweet potatoes. However, many yam varieties are far larger than either potatoes or sweet potatoes.

Yams, which may have originated in West Africa, are grown in tropical regions throughout the world and are the main food of hundreds of millions of people.

This early drawing shows Incas harvesting potatoes in the Andes Mountains of what is now Peru. Dating from about 1565, the drawing comes from a book about the New World.

Potatoes in History

Potatoes long ago became a major food crop in the high country of the Andes—and for very good reasons. In mountain country two miles and more high, subject to frost at all times of the year, few plants—and certainly none of the other major food crops—could survive. Indeed, hardly anything but potatoes would survive and grow well in those conditions.

Potatoes—because they grew underground and were fed by the starch stored in their own roots—did far better than just survive. They became the main food of the Native Americans of the high Andes. Potatoes were also very easy to plant, cultivate, harvest, and store—and all with only simple foot plows that were little more than digging sticks.

Potatoes stored extremely well,

The potato has spread around the world, but it is still also grown in its homeland in the Andes Mountains. Using simple hand tools not far removed from those used in earlier times, these farmers are clearing part of a hillside in Ecuador for planting potatoes.

too. They could last for years in storage, once their water content (75 percent to 80 percent) was removed.

Removing their water was very easy to do and did not require any special tools. Once harvested and out of the ground, potatoes were set out to freeze overnight. The next day, while the potatoes were thawing, the people of the community would all together use their bare feet to stamp out of the potatoes as much water as they could.

The process of freezing, thaw-ing, and stamping out water was repeated for as many days as neces-sary until the water was gone. A dry potato substance was left behind, which the Native Americans called *chuño*.

The chuño became a basic and major part of their diet. It provided flour for baking. It was also eaten on its own, after being softened with water. Most chuño was stored and then eaten throughout the year. Stored chuño could last for many years, right through bad harvests and natural disasters.

The Spread of Potatoes

Potatoes were probably intro-duced into Europe in the mid-1500s, though possibly a little later. No one knows exactly when they first trav-eled across the Atlantic. However, it is likely that they were brought to Spain by returning Spanish ships soon after the Columbus voyages.

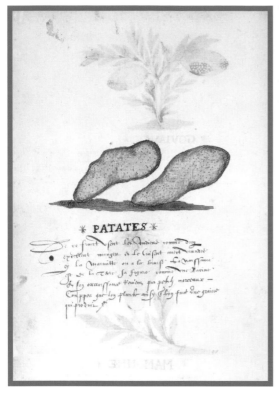

This drawing of sweet potatoes ("Patates") was made in the late 1500s, soon after the Spanish arrived in the Americas. It appeared in a French book, *Natural History of the Indies*. In English the caption reads: "The Indians use this fruit as excellent nourishment. . . ."

being the huge food crop they would later become. This is largely because people thought that potatoes were poisonous—as the green parts of the potato plant are. Many people also believed that potatoes were evil. Potatoes somehow came to be associated with witchcraft, at a time when there was much superstitious fear of witchcraft in Europe.

Potatoes were certainly known and eaten in Spain by 1570, and they were brought to England no later than the 1580s. By the early 1600s they were being cultivated in Spain, Portugal, Italy, France, Germany, Austria, Britain, Ireland, and Britain's American colonies (which included what is now the United States).

Although widely cultivated in Europe, potatoes were still far from

Wild potato plants are much smaller than the modern cultivated potato varieties. However, plant researchers study wild potatoes like these, trying to find ways to improve modern potatoes.

However, although potatoes were unpopular as food, they were widely used as medicines, as were belladonna and other members of the nightshade family.

By the 1800s different times had brought different attitudes and needs to Europe. Most Europeans no longer saw potatoes as evil or associated them with witchcraft. At the same time—and of great importance—Europe's population had grown enormously. The highly nutritious, easy-to-grow potato became one of Europe's major food sources, especially for the poor. In Ireland, for example, farmers could feed a big family on the potatoes they grew on a very small piece of rented land and still have enough money left to pay ground rent to the big landowners. Potatoes soon were seen as a necessity in many countries.

During the 1800s potatoes became part of the basic diet of many Europeans. This British woman is sitting outside her cottage peeling potatoes for the family's meal in a painting by Ernest Walbourn.

Echoes of the 1840s potato famine are still found in many parts of Ireland. This mural painted on the wall of a house in Belfast, Northern Ireland, shows poor women digging for potatoes during the famine.

The Great Irish Potato Famine

In the mid-1850s dependence on the potato for food led to one of the greatest disasters in European history. In the early 1840s the North American potato crop was hit by a disease. The disease was carried across the Atlantic to western Europe in 1845 and partially destroyed the 1845 potato crops in Ireland, Germany, and several other countries. The 1846 and 1847 potato crops were completely destroyed in Ireland and greatly damaged in other European countries. The crop began to

Modern researchers are still examining ways to protect potatoes from disease, which can destroy the potatoes for food, like this potato that is rotting away.

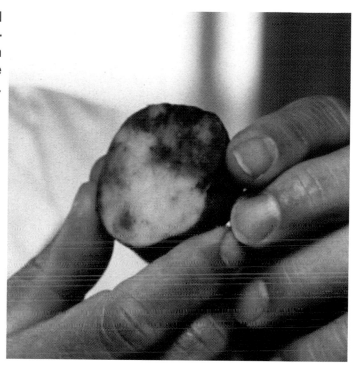

come back in 1848, but by then enormous damage had been done.

The damage was worst by far in Ireland, one of Europe's poorest and most heavily populated countries. In the 150 years between 1690 and 1840, Ireland's population had skyrocketed from 2 million people to more than 8 million. The great majority of these people were very poor farmers who depended on their potato crops to survive.

What we now call "the Great Irish Potato Famine" came quickly in Ireland. After the 1846 crop failed, hungry farm families ate stored potatoes and even the seed potatoes set aside for planting the 1847 crop. Without potatoes to feed

their livestock and their families desperately in need of food, Irish farmers soon slaughtered and ate all their farm animals.

Most of Ireland's farmlands were owned by rich Irish and British landlords. Many of them lived in Britain and took their rent money and profits out of Ireland. Even during the famine, these landowners continued to export and sell food out of Ireland.

During the famine many Irish farmers could not pay their land rents, and the landowners took away their farms. Then millions of homeless Irish farmers wandered the roads, begging for food that did not come.

In many poor areas people still grow their own potatoes. Using a simple shovel (below), this Irish man (left) is digging some white potatoes out of the ground for his own use.

Ireland's poor faced increased poverty, loss of farms, and famine. Since little or no medical help was available, these also brought on killing epidemic diseases. Britain—which then occupied Ireland as a possession—made small and almost useless relief efforts. There were few doctors and nurses and few medical supplies, which were soon used up. Many doctors and nurses were also attacked by disease, making the total situation even worse.

In all, 1 to 1.5 million people died of starvation and plague in Ireland. Some 2 million fled abroad, at least 1.3 million of them to the United States, in the first great wave of Irish-American immigration.

After the potato famine potatoes came back as a major food in Europe and throughout the world. In the United States—with its rich, huge farmlands that produced many kinds of food crops—potatoes never became the kind of major crop they were in Europe.

Peoples in many parts of the world rely on potatoes as a basic food. These are potatoes being sold at a local farmer's market in Guatemala.

Potatoes around the World

Today potatoes are farmed throughout the world, growing best in climates that are cool and damp. They are still grown in the Andean highlands that were their birthplace—and in more varieties there than anywhere else in the world. Yet the great mass of the world's potatoes are now grown elsewhere.

In the centuries after the potato was introduced into Europe from the Americas, the countries of northern Europe became by far the world's greatest potato growers. Potato farming then spread throughout the northern hemisphere. The great mass of the world's potatoes were grown in the huge stretches of land that spread across the northern parts of Europe, Asia, and North America. That remained true until the mid-20th century. As late as the 1960s Europe still produced more than three-quarters of the world's potatoes.

The picture looked very different by the early 21st century. Worldwide potato production has grown—though not nearly as fast as the world's population. Eating habits have changed a good deal in Europe, where most people now eat fewer potatoes and more grains and other foods thought to be healthier than potatoes. At the same time, China, India, and Southeast Asia—

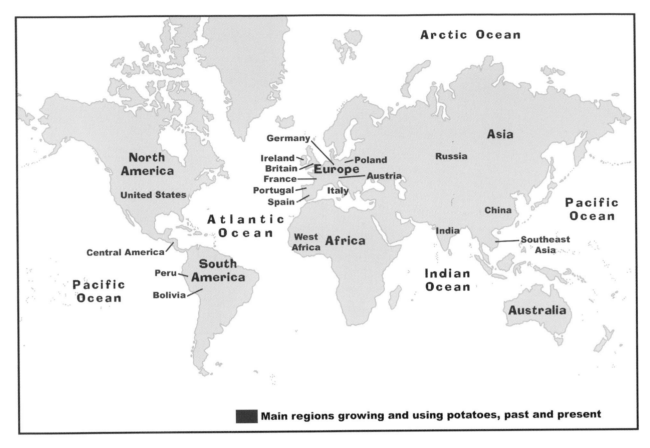

Main regions growing and using potatoes, past and present

in great need of massive new amounts of food to feed their huge and fast-growing populations—are raising much larger amounts of potatoes.

By late in the 20th century China had become the world's largest single potato-producing country, growing four times as many potatoes as it had just 40 years earlier. In the same period Asia as a whole tripled its potato production.

The United States has had a different kind of experience, but even so it has added up to a near-doubling of its potato production.

In the early years of the 21st century only one-third of American potato production is eaten in the form of potatoes as harvested from the fields. Instead, two-thirds is machine-processed, mostly being turned into potato chips, frozen french fries, and many other manufactured potato products.

Today the world's largest potato-producing countries include China, Russia, Poland, the United States, and India. Several other European countries still produce large amounts of potatoes.

This farmer is using a cultivator to work the soil in a potato field. Turning the soil over keeps weeds down and helps air and water reach the all-important roots.

Potato Farming

The basics of potato farming have changed little for many thousands of years. Four thousand years ago, in ancient Peru's high Andes, Native Americans did it all, from planting to harvesting, by hand and with digging sticks. Then with their bare feet, they created edible dried potatoes (chuño) that lasted for years (see p. 12). Modern potato farmers still plant, cultivate, and harvest, following natural laws that have not changed. However, the way farming is done has changed a great deal.

In most of the world the ancient patterns of planting, cultivation,

harvesting, and processing by hand have long since given way to modern potato farming and processing. Today big machines working on large farms produce massive quantities of potatoes. Most of these are taken to large factories for processing into many kinds of potato products. The world's small farmers still grow what, in earlier times, would have been seen as a lot of potatoes. However, the potato crops that now feed billions are mainly coming out of large mechanized farms and factories.

Potatoes can be planted and grown either from small whole

These are "seed potatoes" that have begun to sprout. Each of these sprouts comes from an "eye" of the potato and can grow into a new potato plant.

To grow new potato plants, you can plant a whole potato in the ground or just pieces containing "eyes," which are actually seeds. Here two potato pieces are growing in test tubes. The one in back has already sent up a green sprout, the beginning of a potato plant.

potatoes (*seed potatoes*) or from cut pieces of potato containing its "eyes," which are really its seeds. The potato's many eyes grow near the surface of the potato's skin, and every eye is capable of sprouting into a new potato plant.

Modern potato farmers usually use cut pieces containing two or three eyes for planting, to make sure that a new plant will grow from each piece of potato. They rarely use whole seed potatoes, although these were often used for planting in earlier times.

Planting today is mainly done by machine. Usually the machine handles the whole planting process: plowing the long, straight furrows (trenches) that will receive the potato seeds, planting the seeds, and then covering the planted seeds with earth. How deep and how far apart the seeds are planted depends on the variety of potato being planted, the nature of the land, climate, and many other such factors. These factors also help farmers decide how the potato fields will be prepared to receive the potato seeds.

In temperate climate zones, as in most of the United States and Europe, potatoes have a growing season of three to five months. During that time farmers try to provide the best possible conditions for the healthy growth of the potato plants and their potatoes. Watching over the health of the growing plants, farmers supply water through irrigation as needed and fertilizers to encourage healthy growth. The main fertilizers used in the fields include nitrogen, phosphorus, potassium, and magnesium.

Farmers throughout the world also use a wide range of chemicals (*pesticides*) to kill insect pests, fight plant diseases, and kill unwanted plants in the fields. Some pesticides are applied as sprays from machines in the fields, and others from low-flying airplanes called *crop dusters*.

Though it looks harmless, the Colorado potato beetle (left) can do enormous amounts of damage to potato crops, unless stopped by pesticides or other methods. Because chemical pesticides are often dangerous, some people have been experimenting with less-damaging alternatives. These two sweet potato farmers are spraying a field with a mixture of vegetable oil and dishwashing detergent.

Traditionally potatoes were dug out of the ground by hand, whether in large potato fields or in "kitchen gardens," like this one in Britain, painted by William Small.

Modern pesticides have proven extremely useful to potato farmers—though sometimes at far too great a price. Some pesticides have polluted the environment, damaging people, plants, animals, earth, air, and water. Among these have been such substances as aldrin, parathion, and DDT (dichloro-diphenyl-trichloroethane). Many of these pesticides are now banned in the United States and many other countries, though they are still used in other parts of the world. DDT was the world's most used pesticide before it was banned in the United States in 1972.

Seeking to improve potatoes, modern scientists have been making changes in potato genes, the basic set of biological codes that guide the plant's growth and development.

This *genetic engineering* has developed new varieties of potatoes with attractive characteristics. However, many people fear that changing a plant's genetic codes might damage the environment, including the people who eat the potatoes. The long-term effects of such genetic changes are still unknown.

Harvesting Potatoes

Some small farmers around the world still harvest potatoes by hand. However, potato harvesting today is most often done by machine.

Modern machines handle the entire harvesting process in a single pass. Sometimes working on several rows of potato plants at a time, they dig whole potato plants out of the ground, including the potatoes and the soil around and under the plant, along with anything in that soil, such as stones and other plants.

The harvester gathers up everything. Then the potatoes are separated from all the rest, in a series of processes that shake the potatoes off the potato plants and move them through the harvester into storage containers. Everything else that has been taken into the machine is dropped back onto the potato field.

The harvested potatoes are either stored for future use or moved on directly into their many uses. Some are headed for cooking and current use, such as a potato bought at a supermarket, taken home, and cooked as part of dinner. Most are headed for a potato factory, where they will be prepared and processed into potato chips, frozen french fries, dried potatoes, or any of several other potato products (see p. 26). Wherever headed, most potatoes are stored before use, though some go directly to factories.

Modern harvesting machines scoop up whole potato plants, plus whatever is in the soil immediately around them. Then the potatoes are shaken loose from the rest, which falls back into the field, while the potatoes are moved into storage containers.

Before potatoes can be cooked and eaten, they are cleaned and usually peeled. At home and in fine restaurants, peeling is generally done by hand, using a peeler such as this one. However, in factories the peeling is done by machine, aided by heated water or chemicals.

The Many Uses of Potatoes

When cooked at home, potatoes are generally boiled, baked, or roasted, usually with seasonings and other foods added, such as butter, sour cream, or cheese. Before cooking, potatoes are scrubbed clean and sometimes peeled by hand. However, a very large proportion of the potatoes we eat are processed in factories, especially favorite snacks

such as potato chips and french fries.

When potatoes arrive at the factory, several basic steps are taken right at the start, whatever potato products are being made. First the potatoes are inspected. Potatoes unfit for processing are sorted out and removed, along with unwanted materials from the harvesting pro-

Before potatoes are processed, they go through a cleaning and sorting process, designed to shake potatoes loose of soil and other unwanted material, as on rollers like these.

cess (see p. 24). These include soil, stones, and various kinds of trash, such as cans and other items of metal, twigs and other pieces of wood, plastic, and glass.

The metals are found with metal detectors and magnets. The stones, which are heavier than the potatoes, are removed by floating the potatoes in water. The stones fall to the bottom of the water tank, while the potatoes stay afloat. The wood, which is lighter than the potatoes, rises to the top of the water tank,

and is then separated and removed from the potatoes. The various other kinds of trash are also removed, with clinging bits of plastic hardest of all to separate from the potatoes. Most of the soil and sand on the potatoes is removed by washing and machine brushing.

Peeling is the next major step in preparing potatoes for processing. This is done by machine and can be done in several different ways, depending on the potatoes' variety, age, condition, and the thickness

Potato chips are routinely served with many kinds of foods, especially hamburgers, hot dogs, and various sandwiches.

and hardness of their skin. Some batches of potatoes may be steam-cleaned and lightly cooked to loosen their skins before peeling. Others may only need light machine brushing to remove their skins. Still others may be passed through chemicals that remove their skin and then through steam aimed at cleaning the chemicals from the potatoes.

The last step in preparing the potatoes for manufacturing is to inspect and remove any remaining flawed potatoes and potato parts. Then the potatoes go into the manufacturing process. How they are handled from then on depends on

what kinds of products they will become.

Potato Products

The main kinds of manufactured potato products are *potato chips* and *frozen french fries*, along with several other frozen potato products. There are also several kinds of canned and dried potato products made and sold.

Potato chips are a tremendously popular snack food in many parts of the world. Chips are made by machine-slicing clean, raw, peeled potatoes into thin sections and several different shapes, depending on the kinds of chips being made. The slicers used are big, multibladed machines that cut many slices at a time. The cut slices are then washed in water and air-dried.

The potato slices are then either fried in cooking oil or oven-dried into no-fat chips. Most chips are fried in oil, which is the long-established way of making them. Many different kinds of oils may be used, each of them providing a different kind of taste for the chips made with it.

Many people think that chips made without cooking oil do not taste as good as those fried in cooking oil. On the other hand, they are a lot healthier to eat, for chips and other potato products fried in oil are far more fattening than dried potatoes. That is the main reason that doctors and nutritionists constantly warn about the dangers of eating potato chips, frozen french fries, and other foods fried in oil.

After cooking, most potato chips are salted and seasoned, packaged, and sent to market. "No-salt" po-

tato chips are also made for people who have to limit their salt intake for health reasons.

Frozen french fries are by far the most popular of the frozen potato products. However, there are also several other kinds of frozen potato products, among them frozen mashed potatoes and frozen dinners that include frozen potatoes in various forms. Like most potato chips, frozen french fries are usually fried in cooking oils.

One of the most popular of all "fast foods" are french fries, like those in this bright red package. For health reasons, however, some people bake frozen "fries" instead of frying them in oil.

Words to Know

annual A kind of plant that lives and grows for only one year, unlike a PERENNIAL.

belladonna: See DEADLY NIGHTSHADE.

carbohydrates Chemical compounds (mixed substances) made of the elements (basic substances) carbon, hydrogen, and oxygen. Found in the cells of every living thing, they are necessary to human life. The carbohydrates in potatoes include STARCH and several sugars.

chuño A dry, edible potato substance made by Native Americans in South America's high Andes Mountains thousands of years ago.

crop dusters Low-flying airplanes that spray PESTICIDES on farmlands and crops.

DDT (dichloro-diphenyl-trichloroethane) A highly toxic (poisonous) PESTICIDE. Now banned in the United States and many other countries, it was once the most widely used pesticide in the world.

deadly nightshade (belladonna) A member of the NIGHTSHADE FAMILY that is especially deadly because it carries large amounts of the natural poison SOLANINE.

Dioscorea: See YAMS.

dry matter (solid matter) The portion of a potato left after its water has been removed. All of the potato's nutrition is in its dry matter.

edible Suitable for eating.

eyes: See SEED POTATOES.

Great Irish Potato Famine A disastrous Irish famine and plague of the mid-1840s, following the failure of the 1846 and 1847 potato crops because of potato disease.

harvester A farming tool used to harvest growing plants, from the earliest handheld farming tools to complicated, high-powered modern harvesting machines.

Irish potato A white-fleshed kind of potato that is the world's main potato crop. There are many varieties of the Irish potato.

Ipomoea batatas: See YAMS.

nightshade family (Solanaceae) A family of plants that includes the potato plant (SOLANUM TUBEROSUM) and DEADLY NIGHTSHADE.

peeling Several ways of removing potato skins during the manufacture of potato products.

perennial A kind of plant that remains alive and regrows year after year, unlike an ANNUAL.

pesticides Chemicals used to kill insect pests, fight plant diseases, and kill unwanted plants in fields. Some pesticides have proven very useful, but some have also poisoned people and polluted the environment, damaging plants, animals, earth, air, and water. (See also DDT.)

plow To cut long, straight furrows (trenches) to prepare a farm field for planting. Also the kind of tool used to cut the furrows.

proteins Basic chemical compounds found in potatoes that are necessary to human life. All proteins contain carbon, nitrogen, oxygen, hydrogen, and special substances called *amino acids*.

rhizomes Substems of those parts of the potato plant stem that grow underground, from which potatoes grow.

root plants: See TUBERS.

seed potatoes (*Ipomoea batatas*) Small whole potatoes or cut pieces of potatoes containing "eyes" (seeds). Either can be used for planting new potato plants.

Solanaceae: See NIGHTSHADE FAMILY.

solanine A natural poison that grows in the above-ground parts of all the plants in the NIGHTSHADE FAMILY, including potatoes. Because solanine was identified with the nightshade family, some Europeans thought potatoes to be poisonous when they were first brought to Europe.

Solanum tuberosum The scientific name of the potato plant.

solid matter: See DRY MATTER.

starch A kind of CARBOHYDRATE, a nutrient (nourishing substance) found in potatoes.

sweet potatoes (*Ipomoea batatas*) Edible TUBERS that look like and are often mistaken for potatoes and YAMS. Sweet potatoes are actually part of the morning glory plant family.

tubers Tubelike portions of plant stems, among them potatoes. From these grow seed-bearing new plants of the same kind. Potatoes are often mistakenly called *root plants*, but they also have root systems, which are inedible.

yams Edible TUBERS that look like and are often mistaken for potatoes or SWEET POTATOES, but actually come from a different plant family (*Dioscorea*).

On the Internet

The Internet has many interesting sites about potatoes. The site addresses often change, so the best way to find current addresses is to go to a search site, such as www.yahoo.com. Type in a word or phrase, such as "potato."

As this book was being written, websites about potatoes included:

http://www.cipotato.org/index2.asp
International Potato Center, a site of the major international institute studying potatoes (and sweet potatoes) and how to improve them, including a multimedia history: (http://www.cipotato.org/potato/History/routes/frame.htm)

http://lanra.dac.uga.edu/potato/
World Geography of the Potato, a site from the University of Georgia discussing history and growing of potatoes in countries around the world.

http://www.urbanext.uiuc.edu/veggies/potato1.html
Watch Your Potato Grow, a website on growing potatoes from the University of Illinois.

http://www.idahopotato.com/
Idaho Potato Commission website.

http://www.mainepotatoes.com/
Maine Potato Board website.

In Print

Your local library system will have various books on potatoes. The following is just a sampling of them.

Baker, H. G. *Plants and Civilization*. Belmont, CA: Wadsworth, 1978.
Burton, W. G. *The Potato*. New York: John Wiley, 1989.
Cox, A. B. *The Potato*. London: W. H. Collingridge, 1967.
Fenton, Carroll Lane, and Herminie B. Kitchen. *The Plants We Live On*. New York: John Day, 1971.
Foods of Plant Origin. D. K. Salunkhe and S. S. Deshpande, eds. New York: Van Nostrand, 1991.
Franck, Irene M., and David M. Brownstone. *The Green Encyclopedia*. New York: Prentice Hall, 1992.
Gould, Wilbur A. *Potato Production, Processing, and Technology*. Timonium, MD: CTI Publications, 1999.
Heiser, Charles B. *Seed to Civilization*. San Francisco: W. H. Freeman, 1971.
Lang, James. *Notes of a Potato Watcher*. College Station, TX: Texas A & M Press, 2001.
Meltzer, Milton. *The Amazing Potato*. New York: HarperCollins, 1992.
Pyke, Magnus. *Food Science and Technology*. London: John Murray, 1981.
Roberts, Jonathan. *The Origins of Fruits and Vegetables*. New York: Rizzoli, 2001.
Salaman, Redcliffe N. *The History and Social Influence of the Potato*. Cambridge, UK: Cambridge University Press, 1949.
Selsam, Millicent E. *The Plants We Eat*. New York: Morrow, 1981.
Silverstein, Alvin, and Virginia B. Silverstein. *Potatoes*. Englewood Cliffs, NJ: Prentice Hall, 1976.
Talbert, William F., and Ora Smith. *Potato Processing*. Westport, CT: AVI Publishing, 1975.
Van Nostrand's Scientific Encyclopedia, 8th ed., 2 vols. Douglas M. Considine and Glenn D. Considine, eds. New York: Van Nostrand Reinhold, 1995.
Vaughan, J. G., and C. A. Geissler. *The New Oxford Book of Plants*. New York: Oxford, 1997.
Zuckerman, Larry. *Potato*. New York: North Point, 1998.

Index